Expecting Songbirds
Selected Poems
1983-2015

Expecting Songbirds
Selected Poems
1983-2015

Joe Benevento

2015 © Joe Benevento
ISBN: 978-0-944048-66-5
purple flag press online at vacpoetry.org/purple-flag
Cover and interior design by forgetgutenberg.com

For my wife, Carol
and our children,
Maria, Joseph, Claire and Margaret.

Contents

from Holding On

from Willing To Believe

from My Puerto Rican Past

from Tough Guys Don't Write

from Ode to Pears
(Uncollected Published Poems)

from
Holding On

First Sighting of the Man-in-the Moon

We three stood in the stars,
black sky, full yellow moon
of Midwest July, remembering.
Silencing the jokes of the party
we'd just left, the night,
resembling too well our sorrow,
pulled us to speak of a mutual friend
so suddenly changed: self-destructive,
overcome.

Perhaps to temper our hopelessness,
we sought out constellations,
signs there above.
When Allison felt the man-
in-the-moon's eyes upon us,
she pointed him out, but Raphael
confessed he had never been able
to see that face, never understood
the other children's belief.
Allison and I, patient
in our understanding,
mapped out for Ray what made
that mass of yellow rock a man,
found eyebrows, cratered nose,
dark lips, gave to him our youth,
imaginings, till he felt them too
and almost cried out for joy,
while that lunatic moon embraced the light
from the eyes of all its children.

Felipa Gatos

Phyllis Katz, your eyes defined blue
black hair whispered when you walked
your figure full as flowers in an extravagant
bouquet, your smile innocence and mischief
married and divorced.

That name the Nicaraguan girl
in our Latin American novels course
gave to you, Felipa Gatos, fit well:
silly and sensual at once,
hurting and delighting
as only a pun can, as you did
the day your best friend Margie
skipped and you told me to take
her seat beside you.

We joked, intimated all class long
while Echeverría wondered why
he ever left Uruguay, why no one
cared about Los Pasos Perdidos.
I, for one, enchanted beyond repair
when your long hair brushed my hand
or you whispered words made magical
to me, never wanted to retrace my steps,
though now I feel lost remembering
that path, Felipa, and the way we
danced with a cat-like grace
from the pulse of your laughing blue eyes.

Holding On

Some oak trees keep half or more
than half their leaves into winter,
even though those leaves are dead
and brown, even though the trees
will have to let them go before new
ones may green their stubborn limbs again.

I have lived with oak trees all my life;
there are some in front of my office
window now, clutching bits of January
ice and snow in a sullen lethargy of leaves,
but I never was aware how they held on
to death until I bought a house in May,
waited for my oak trees to unleaf
so I could cart death off all at once
in dark garbage bags.

Now I wait patiently for April,
knowing those leaves must come down,
however long winter seems to linger,
knowing life is at least as inevitable
as dying; their place is on the ground
rotting a solemn song
of cycles and seasons.

Work Song

For you, Eric Martinborough, stock-boy, age 33
and all those ways of looking busy doing nothing.
Randy Diamond, order picker,
effective and fast till the 10:15 jay.
Woodie the freight elevator operator,
any time a "good time for a cold one."
Judge Franklyn ("That's his real name?") the porter:
"Working hard?" "Hardly working."
Jorge Irizarry the checker
and his drunken dreams of Puerto Rican paradise.
Mario, my first foreman,
dead from a stress-induced stroke.

Lucky and Pedro of the "Thunderfucks,"
knife-wielding, motorcycle plumbers.
The Attica Alumni, The Rehab 7,
cold Buds standard equipment,
OTB required outside reading,
Skip, their valedictorian
still wistful about his lost "38"
because shooting is
"just like coming."

All of my amigos in physical labor,
the knowing painful smiles,
the macho covers. Practiced
invulnerability or the nervous jingle
of those who know they aren't
fooling anybody.
Like Robert wearing his suit and NY Times
on the subway, while the factory smell
gives him up for pretend middle-class
or John who brags about stealing Cadillacs
while on "ludes" and then is taken off
by some pato Cuban half his size,
with a baseball bat and louder voice,
John's hammer hanging limp from his tool belt.

Nothing sweeter than the sound of: "Break time,
want anything from the store?"
except the way your watch ticks louder
around 10 to 5 on Fridays, and Judge,
his breath reeling with cheap beer,
proclaiming the just destruction of another week
of pain: "Another day, another dollar, and Monday
can't have us tonight."

Protection

My friend Isál, the sinister collie, warned me
of Weird Sarah's approach from the other side
of the tall weeds and shit we were strolling through;
her maroon-lipped, pent-up like piss desire
cut short by his foaming devotion.

Home also unsafe: the embarrassment
of my mother confronting relentless Sarah,
her apron stained with macaroni blood, commanding:
"Keep your hands off my boy!"

Seeking sanctuary at José's and Sylvia's home:
their parents out punishing bingo boards,
José out pimping worms.
Sylvia ushers me in;
her long whips like hair, her short voice dripping
sticky, liquid lust as she desires me
to help write her history paper.

I hesitate, she approaches, glinting reward,
her silver shorts rasping with each rhythmic step.
But José plunges in, green eyes exploding,
loosing me with a look and jamming the controls
with the macabre indignation of his eyebrows
which seem to chant:

In our homeland
we never dined
on close friends
of the family.

Ferry

My father, who labored with honest, calloused
hands, had enough threat in his deep, ever-gruff
voice to make hitting us unnecessary,
my father, taciturn, fatigued from fifty-hour
weeks of constructing other people's houses,
airports, offices,
my dad, who would spend most of his not-free
time sleeping on the couch or doing the many chores
my mother directed his way, stole a Saturday
somehow in the spring to take me
and two of my just older sisters on a subway
ride (we had no car) to lower Manhattan
there to board the Staten Island Ferry
for a nickel apiece, to get our first
look at the Statue of Liberty,
our first voyage on a boat of any sort,
this economical adventure even our family
of nine could afford.

Yet I remember most its extravagance,
the generous ocean tales my father
unfolded into our eager ears,
his voice softer, kinder than we'd known,
his pointing to the yellow buoys and gently
explaining how they helped sound the depths
of the water, the depths of his love
he lavished on us the whole day.
He bought each of us a little gift
on the Staten Island side,
mine a clown doll I cherished
not because I cared about clowns
but because it always smiled to me
a memory to chide away the sometimes
sadness of growing up with a man too hard
worked to very often share the wealth
of oceans, fictions and other necessary gifts.

Prince of the Sun God

When I was a child of nine-
teen, I used to dazzle my companions
by predicting with sobering accuracy
when it would and would not rain.
Most took it for a joke, a damned good one,
since at my peak I predicted
the only day in eleven when it would
not rain. Our Spanish Club picnic depended
on it; it was cloudy as rain all day,
but I just let a few drops fall
to ferret out the unbelievers, leaving
them dry while I ate fried chicken
with a look linked to hubris.
I kidded my girlfriend I was
The Prince of the Sun God and that this
was only the beginning of my miracles;
in our most hormonal moments she was willing
to wager I could call on the light
like a friend.

Now she knows better; we've been
married ten years; I get wet all the time
going umbrellaless into partly cloudy.
I am occasionally tempted
to shake my fist at my father,
but looking at him straight on
dazzles and hurts and we always
knew it was just a joke, anyway.

Alone

That red-eyed sun sets remorselessly
into evening, leaving willows, poplars
to the uneven devices of night;
owls alert to their killing hours,
their prey knowing no better,
making itself available to death.
This is the only truth worth
considering, how night never
really falls, how we are
the descent; under cover of darkness
we procreate, ashamed of our lust
for loss, lacking always the will
it takes to sit stoically
with solitude, never once
needing to curse
that single life-
giving yellow star
of our solitary lives.

What Our Love Could Be Like

"Dejando mi cuidado,
entre las azucenas, olvidado."
—San Juan de la Cruz, "Noche Oscura"

If I could find a God-
like love, overpowering
emotions, physical essence
so completely I could
leave behind my caution
to a field of lilies, experience,
even for a minute that sensation
of well-being, being well
beyond the touch of guilt,
second, third thoughts,
I would adhere to that love like
the perfume of cherry blossoms
in the center of an enormous orchard,
I would be more faithful than death,
become a saint to passion,
turn your worries to flowers,
fruit, gathering, carrying
all of our delicious burdens
for the chance
to love that way.

Richmond Hill Street Blues

The rhythm's changed.
That bad walk we worked to be safe
in the streets don't work no more.

The rhythm's changed.
Indian girls that ought to wear
bindis and saris instead
strut the streets of Queens
in heavy make-up and designer jeans.

The rhythm's changed.
I'm lost within familiar things:
Freddie's Fish Market, Tunick's Department Store
and José's and Kerry's houses
inhabited by strangers.

The rhythm has changed
and I can hardly revive her image,
how she looked that winter evening
a beautiful Creole vision, dancing
off the bus with her, "Hello, Joseph,"
as if I had been waiting for her alone
and have been ever since.

The rhythm has changed.

She stood there brown as autumn, changed
as autumn, she stood, laughing with me
in the sunlight of our backyard and new puppy.
He's dead now, and they tell me she is dying.

New York is forever dying.
The honeysuckle and roses
in my mother's front yard
are lying. They seem the same
and pretend to ignore the syncopation,
diffusing decay with their ignorant fragrance.

The rhythm's changed.
She steps beyond me now,
and I never got to dance with her,
not even when I almost knew how to dance,
before, the rhythm, changed.

Hallene After Divorce

Was the mini-skirt merely the latest fashion,
something she threw on casually, without reflection?
Or was it for the world to see the lost weight, lost
worries, beauty more heart-stabbing than ever?

Or was it all and only for me?
So that I might look at her more
closely, might sweat from her new,
dangerous status, might wish to hold her
desire in my arms, might long to add
a dash of lust to spice out the Platonic
flame I've been lying by all these years.

Your New Boyfriend

Dresses all in leather, has
blue-black spiked hair; they tell me
he works in a grocery store,
plays nights in an old-new
wave band; doesn't talk
much, a small-town-punk-Gary
Cooper, I guess.
He does not converse
pointedly on Whitman
or Salinger, Borges or
Malamud, as we would,
will not appreciate
the nuances of your Ph.D. panics,
but, you keep telling your friends,
he makes you happy, fulfills
you in the racy way
of almost strangers, some
indifferently handsome
guy who mistakes you
for a floozy in the sometimes
biker bar, and is more than willing
to keep on making
that same mistake
the rest of your
happy lives.

Fictions

"A lover's a liar
To himself he lies.
The truthful are loveless,
Like oysters their eyes."
—Kurt Vonnegut Jr., Cat's Cradle

What I tell myself in the tea-rose-
colored morning, your sleeping
form beside me breathes in readily
like any dream.
Only loss is real,
and only love conceals
the harshness of this movement
unwavering from the living
fragrance of flowers.
Gather these soft vows
while you trust, all life
is sad unsowing; no one
can console this forever,
nobody with sense would
be willing to admit sunset's
colors are fiercer, finer rapture,
leading us to darkness, good
night.
Should I say "I love you"
to your sleeping
beauty, these tears absolve
the dream unloved
truth knows to be-
lie.

Aftermath

Like a stranger she keeps
to a corner of the bed
and caresses her pillow
with soft, yellow hair.
The ends of the darkness
dissolve near the window,
half-moon and lonely stars;
she hardly stirs,
just breathes lightly
to make me aware
her rancor is alive
her hate's not unfastened,
her eyes are yet open
to the edge of despair.

Poem for Me

It came over me in a particularly mordant
moment of self-
pity: I have never once been subject,
object, nor even pale preposition of any-
one's poetry.
I who have written poems
for ten times more women
than I have ever
touched, I who once saved
Victor Torrent's life with a song
he carried months later in his pocket
instead of those pills, I
who have been told more
than twice that the sonnet
I delivered was the first
in some lonely woman's life
who had been waiting
(we all wait) to be a star,
shadow for fourteen lines,
have never inspired any-
one to feel
enough to want
to put me
on paper,
never had
the kind of effect
dozens and dozens
of you have willed
onto me, wondering
like a vagrant in a realm
without response, darkly
seeking reciprocity
that never announces itself
in so many
words.

Her First Bill Fish

A white marlin,
"the highlight of my summer,"
she informed me in the same letter
she confessed to having less
than no excuse for missing
me in New York in May after
we had supposedly arranged things.

She took off for Florida instead,
disappearing for twelve days,
"not a good idea," but, there it's
done and she figured I had "had it"
with her so that's why she didn't
call to apologize or explain, but

hey, it's been a "rough time" for
her, and, of course, only these friends
of mine, the pretty ones with messed up
love lives and big fish to fry have rough lives,
not us simple forgivers who are readily baited,
easily hauled in, and anxious to be mounted.

Departure From La Plata

The train swallowed you whole
and, I swear, in seven seconds
wished you from present to past tense.

Now that you've been gone a few days
you'd think there'd have to be more left
than the vestige of that powerful train
devouring you.

Has it come to this?
Is it true what you implied
by not finding the damned window
in time to wave good-bye?

Across Nevada

"The loneliest road in America"
needs no self-proclaiming signs.
When you travel State Route 50
you will find no town,
gas station, traffic
for fifty, seventy, as many
as ninety miles at a stretch.
In the summer the intense shimmer
off the blacktop can be intoxicating;
you have to look left to the unyielding
desert, right to lifeless hills,
or, rarely, straight ahead to a significant
side-winding snake to remember
this is a real road, real world at all.

The cruise control set at 75 or so,
the radio off, air conditioner
working, it is as close to being
on automatic pilot as you can ever
get in an automobile.
You will suppose you can make Eli
with ease, but thankfully stop
long before at Eureka, strip-mined
almost off the map, a place
even ghosts won't haunt,
just to get beyond that loneliness,
just to see the almost human faces
of dead town depression.

You will remember the opening of
a favorite poem: "Afoot and light-hearted
I take to the open road," and think, with all
the ruefulness of the disenchanted: "Walt
Whitman never took a desert; his poem
works as far, perhaps, as Pennsylvania."
If I were you I'd mitigate my solitude,
take a companion, someone you trust,
across that shimmering silver state.

Sunset In Iowa

The only reason we reached the Quad cities
near five was the combination of sleet
and snow near Pittsburgh the day before
that slid us off Interstate 80
into a safe motel.
We would have been home
in Missouri, not on the road
four hours away from motion-
less security.
We would have missed the clouds on fire,
the way the horizon rode red and purple
against the snow-covered, lifeless earth,
a promise of distant bounty.
We woke up in our car for the first
time in many days, witnessed the way
the light confirms its purpose
before letting the darkness
drive its time.

Apples

I

April in Richmond Hill, Queens:
the fluttering white essence
of apple blossoms scents our backyard
with fragrant promise, hints of warmer
days ahead, even as the soft petals
pile on the grass, pretending
to be snowfall.

II

August under the apple tree:
I gather small, fallen fruit,
whack it with my baseball bat
over our fence into the vacant lot:
organic home runs I spray into the distance;
juicy volleys that often bless me
as they depart.

I rarely climb high enough
for finer fruit, leave
that to my brothers,
invading neighbor kids,
though I enjoy the tart results
of their death-defying rambles.
Every summer into fall the tree delivers,
we gather its offerings, enjoy our mother's
pies, though less each year
we grow older, until the worms
take over, the very wood falters,
the tree dies because we do not know
how to care for it.
My father chops it down, leaving
only a stump to stand in complaint
of our neglect.

III

October in East Lansing:
three couples, all graduate students
at Michigan State, agree to an autumn
road trip, drive to an apple orchard
to see how cider is made,
to eat hot doughnuts soaked in it,
to enjoy the colors of dying
leaves on the way.

Six highly educated people
are amazed by pomace,
"the pulpy refuse" after
apple pressing; it resembles
cardboard except for the lingering
apple odor; the owner tells us
cattle love it.

We think we understand transience.
As students we expect not to have
many opportunities for autumn
treks together, but nothing we read
in the ripe orchard warns us,
not one of our marriages will last:
Connecticut, California, Nevada, Georgia,
Minnesota and Missouri each holds one
of those six travelers, scattered
like dead leaves to the four winds.

IV

February just outside Kirksville, Missouri:
my newlywed notices the house
we have agreed to purchase
has a few crab apples dormant
on its 3.2 acres of mostly oaks.
She murmurs regret, wishes
they could grow fruit large enough to eat.
At first I think to tell her color,
tart fragrance are all we want
from apple trees, remembering hours
of careful youth wasted at work
with a knife in search of worms.
Instead, I sniff the way cinnamon's smell
swirls with apples in the oven
of a piecrust, recall how even discarded
skins, stems, seeds scream with happy apple
life, remember the pale green, soft yellow,
blotchy red of fruit more honest as you take it
from its source, and say: "Maybe we'll plant
a few ourselves; we have the room,
the time to try."

from
Willing To Believe

The A Train: Take It or Leave It

My friend Frank was afraid
to ride the subway; like me
he had to take the A from Queens,
where it starts above ground,
along Liberty Avenue, passing storefronts,
sycamores, and, finally, a cemetery before
descending into the bowels of Brooklyn:
East New York, Bed-Sty, Brooklyn Heights,
then on to Manhattan, where I got off
downtown, West 4th, for NYU, while
Frank sweated it almost to its limits
on past Harlem to Manhattan College.

I wasn't any tougher than Frank,
a little taller, but skinny
and four-eyed, no threat
to make a potential mugger hesitate
the slightest moment, but I guess
I had surer things to worry about,
matters that might be a bit
more within my control: like getting
Hallene Lieteau or Dorothy Lin to like me;
or memorizing enough about photosynthesis
not to flunk the next Biology exam.

Frankie fretted, postured, flinched:
he got robbed before freshman year
was out, though the muggers were polite,
hardly showed their knives, let him keep
his wallet after they emptied it of its
measly three dollar take.

I rode the A for four years, back
and forth to school, a summer factory job,
late night NYU mixers, without incident.
Frank's folks bought him a car.

Junior's Problem

Junior Normandía was a lot whiter than me,
but I'm only talking about skin
color and maybe those blue eyes of his
that had him looking some like
that loco judío, Jerry Lewis,
a suggestion Junior hated even more
than me not being Puerto Rican.

We were friends together on 130th Street
with José, Fernando, Ricardo, Kerry, Mike,
me the only one not Latino or black,
just a Wop not convincing anyone
but my best boys that I belonged,
though to myself I laughed:
the word Latin came from Italy,
though Cicero and those other dead white
dudes I was trying to decipher
at Cathedral Prep didn't know a thing
about plátanos fritos, much less
how to merengue.

José, Kerry, Mike I grew up with
since second grade, but Junior
he came later
to our all-of-a-sudden a barrio,
from Brighton Beach, where he'd learned
to hate Caucasians.
Our love of baseball, hoops, chicas,
singing, goofing together, plus the way
the rest of our group all treated
me like blood, was enough to keep us tight
for a few years, but he finally could not take
having a blanco brother, had to tip
away to Tony, Miguel, Victor, the bad

boys of our vecindario. They took him
to drugs, helped him ruin his life:
that beautiful guy who really had a rap,
who always had your back, who made you
happy to be alive, left us for good
and thirty years later, somehow
I still feel responsible for his hate.

Pigeon Party

When I was young, long-haired
and living in New York, I worked
in a factory on the edge of Greenwich
Village. Sometimes to escape the smell
of that place, its faint filtering of asbestos
particles (from item #42-309, sheets
which we packed, innocent
of their cancerous intent) I'd stroll
to Washington Square Park, eat my lunch
in the open air, observing the park life:
old men playing chess; young musicians, like
myself, though unencumbered by factory smells;
once a pretty Moonie, who said I looked forlorn,
thought she could help.
Another time I saw a lawyer type lunching
while giving hell to his wife
(I saw no ring, but guys like that usually
treat their girlfriends better.) It got so
bad she got up crying. He stayed steaming
in three pieces of suit, intent on finishing
his meal.
As I was leaving, I dropped half my sandwich
at his feet, knowing a stream of ever present
pigeons would swoop over to molest him
with their scavenging. He cursed their whir
of feathers, beaks, hunger; as he rushed
up he spilled some soda on his pants.
I laughed to myself, found my factory
afternoon whirring by more rapidly
than ever before, was still chuckling
at 5, down the subway steps back to Queens.
Twenty years later, though my hair
is short, and I even have occasion
to wear a suit, I can't see a pigeon
without being at least
a little happy.

Things To Come

Six year old boy, red hair, blue eyes,
with a green alligator, pseudo-surf board toy,
hovers patiently around me and my two-year
old Maria, in the very shallow waters
of the lake, where she can sit with her head
out of harm's way.
Finally, he begins: tells us he's no mere
local, is in from Texas, recalls fishing
for sand dollars in the Gulf Coast, catching
hundreds of them, asks if Maria's white, plastic
sand sifter is a minnow catcher.
His attention to my little girl
seems explained by his own three year old
sister who isn't with him at the beach,
but when I take Maria out to deeper
water, in part to lose his loquaciousness,
she asks about him, says she likes that boy,
and when we revisit him back in the shallows
he demonstrates the proper way of floating,
wonders if Maria knows how yet,
then offers to loan her his alligator,
letting my girl touch the hard
plastic teeth he claims can hurt
your leg if they should scrape against it.
A moment later he tells me:
"Your daughter has a pretty voice,"
and in her recounting this day's adventures
to her mother, she's prouder of that compliment
than the bluegill we almost caught
in her green bucket, the way she kicked
her feet with Daddy holding her safe
in the deep water, the beautiful fawn
we almost hit on the way home.
Maria is sleeping now, may be dreaming already
of red hair, lake-blue eyes.

On the Rights of Women Not to Have to Sleep with Creeps

> *"The lady doth protest too much, me thinks."*
> —Shakespeare, Hamlet

You see them everywhere,
in Yuppie bars, country dives
down to view their self-
satisfied faces: they are the egoists,
tough guys women love.
Not all women, just the ones
who cannot get accustomed to not
seeing wistfulness for weakness,
confusion for corruption of malepower
that one can at least employ, enjoy-
ing still the suggestion that here
in my munificent eye-
balls are answers to questions
you haven't even considered yet,
girlie. Early in the dawn-
ing of that new day we don't
hear so much about anymore, some
woman is going to stand up
yelling, not at those
idiots who leer at her
across a crowded
rumor of sexual
gratifications, but to her
sisters stepping on each
other's feet to get first
in line for the fleecing:
golden days begin when you can
stop expecting Prince Charming
to pop you and care later
about the size of your slipper.

Willing To Believe

Let me pretend you weren't drunk at all,
just now finally brave enough to try
my anger for all the unanswered mail,
years waiting for your never return call.
At 1 A.M. your voice is like a wall
of memory; it makes me want to buy
all your excuses, flowers from the trail
of something big, before time turned it small.
Let me pretend your love to be as real
as three hours you spent reminding me
of what you used to be in my young life.
That way I can cherish what I still feel,
as something beyond what any eye can see,
you far more than some drunk who woke my wife.

The Aroma of Loss

My wife's friend, her husband
seven year itched hard enough
to scar her with an "I don't love
you anymore."
Weeks later the logic of that revelation
took her to a lawyer, apartment hunting
away from their once comfortable home.
In the midst of it all, we had her over
plenty, careful not to further undo her,
if even by some inadvertent reminder of how
sad her life suddenly had become.
I came home one evening to find her
and my spouse listening to Italian
music, which my wife never does voluntarily:
since neither of them understood the words,
there was no way the songs could bring up
an unpleasant association, memory, make
her cry, from words about untrue love, real
loss.
One of the tunes they did not comprehend
was a Neopolitan standard, " 'A tazza 'e café"
a song about a cup of coffee, I translated,
expecting no consequence.
A few days later when she told me she could not
see, taste or smell coffee without feeling
melancholy, I thought it a clever joke; now
I am less certain, since Saturday night
when my wife took her shopping to help her
try to clutter her new, bare apartment,
she bought a coffee pot, a grinder, filters
and three kinds of beans. Her small place
is now fragrant with regret, as if
she suspected all along that foreign song
was really about loss, about missing
the familiar, the irretrievable past,
as if she breathed in that sorrow
without needing to understand
a single word.

Lucy's Confidant

As her best friend here in Missouri
I'm supposed to substitute for the few
lifelong girlfriends back in Statesboro,
so I was the first to learn Alessandro
wanted a divorce, the first to hear
how chiropractor Hank complimented her
and had really good hands, how architect
Turner was too sharp for her own good,
never able to leave thinking for passion's sake.
Today she closes my office door so she can
reenact her first night with her newest guy—
some Waspy name I can't now recall—
but I'll never forget how he held her,
rubbed her back, up and down while they danced,
because Lucy felt compelled to demonstrate,
her own good hands trying to communicate
on me just exactly how this guy worked.

Perhaps this takes friendship too far,
not because any of it was erotic
for either of us; it was more clinical,
or stagey maybe, like two people practicing
a part in some regional theatre romance,
but I still think she should save those moves
for her new lover, or at least her old
pals when she's next in Georgia.
I'm a married man; I do not want
to be reminded how electric the right
touch can be, how the sudden rush of love
will spin the world around faster than
a severe thunderstorm can
become a tornado.
She should definitely keep my
distance the next time
she confides the conflicts,
the conquests
in her single
romantic life.

Does The Holy Ghost Really Like Red?

The priest wears blood
red vestments on Pentecost Sunday
to represent the tongues of flame
said to have appeared over each
of Christ's apostles.
At our church the people who print
the weekly Bulletin "encouraged" all
parishioners to wear red for Pentecost
to honor the lowest profile member of the Trinity.

Really, what normal Catholic
looks for the Holy Spirit past Pentecost
or the mention he gets in the "Glory Be,"
even though he is supposed to be
every bit as much God as the Father
or Son: each of them has half a Christian
Bible devoted to his exploits—
the ghost mere shadows of mention.
About thirty years ago English speaking
Catholics were "encouraged" to start calling him
the "Holy Spirit," so as not to scare children
with a ghost for a God, so as to engender more
respect than a cousin of Casper could expect.

But no change of name or wearing of red
can help. People understand the tough love
of a father, the sacrifice of sons, but spirit—
that eludes them—so much so that their
religion needs fathers, sons, blessed mothers.
Pentecost Sunday the priest should wear purple—
not the somber, sad purple of Lent—
but the ethereal kind at the edge of some butterfly
wings, the shadowy shade a bit of sunshine
sends through light fog, the soft violet
of the ineffable, the never really
knowable, the spirit of holy uncertainty
no organized religion will ever encourage
anyone to love.

Train Trouble

All the years I rode the subway solo
from Richmond Hill to Bay Ridge, where
Carmen waited, or to the Village,
where school and work resided, all
those late nights back from parties
or the graveyard shift at the Daily News,
(when my Uncle Louie could get me on)
I never once was hassled by anyone
but cops: a sarcastic response
to my guileless request for directions
to the IRT; a command I get my butt
off the steps (the benches were crowded
and I was tired) a wake-up shake
on the 2 A.M, A: "Where ya headed, chief?"
"Huh, what?"
"Where ya headed—ya miss ya stop?"
"No, I'm taking it to the end, Lefferts Boulevard."
"Well, keep your head up, get me?"
Later my older brother, a Narc himself,
told me the man was just watching out for me:
one style of muggers specialized in subway sleepers,
going through their pockets,
only cutting those who awoke to protest.
Still, I slept a hundred times before
on the subway, dozens times more after
and the only cut I recall—
that wise ass who asked me did I know how to read,
his billy-club insulting my shoulders before
pointing to the sign for the #2 train,
speeding me away from his public servant
sneer, defining forever how safe I'd feel
whenever I'd spot
a transit cop.

When Senility Comes, Please, No Poetry

I'm reading lots of poems lately
by middle-aged, guilt-laden children,
lines composed in no kind of tranquility,
after another Sunday's return from the nursing
home.
There are some strong images,
an occasionally surprising turn
of phrase, but mostly those words
wear as predictably as time itself,
leaving me less with sympathy
more the unkind desire
to look these people up to plead:
"Leave your parents out of your laments,
particularly those you prepare for publication.
Aren't they suffering enough
not to have to suspect their frail forms
wander through vain efforts
to make something out of what they can
no longer be?"

Better to die young than to remain
a burden on a generation
of children unable to love
without self-indulgent reflection,
better I keep my own sensitive
seven year old away from poetry
writing, so she will only offer
her old man chocolate, some other
forbidden item to ease her way past
another afternoon of my
deeply vacant eyes.

Of Meatballs and Diphthongs

The food at the Olive Garden is not
the worst I've ever eaten; a few of their
desserts are good, even, though their
sauces are solely satisfactory,
and if their breadsticks were people
they would be ashamed of themselves.
Still, their corporation most upsets
my stomach with their TV spot
starting with an Italian-
looking young man introducing us
to "My grandfather, Giovanni."
A very Italian name they have chosen,
certainly, except this supposed paisan'
pronounces his nonno's name wrong,
giving Gio two syllables, Ge-o, like the little
car, instead of the proper, single Jo
of Giovanni.

A silly quibble, some might say,
but the whole advertisement pushes
how authentically Italian the Olive
Garden is, so much so that ol' grandpa
loves it, so much so that they can end
with a slogan: "When you're here, you're
family," though I'm thinking, any Italian
family I've ever eaten with never charged me
for the food, or mispronounced my
grandfather's name.

This Garden Plot

"I dreaded that first robin so."
—Emily Dickinson

In these once subsuming shadows
I suspect crocus, grape hyacinth,
early indications of daffodil, iris,
though the dirt is still
covered by the deaths of many
leaves, yet the green imagines itself
future flowers, ignores the real Northern
Missouri possibilities of late March
frost or even pounds of snow.
Last year only one daffodil made it
to its bright yellow conclusion,
screaming springtime in the faceless
faces of so many of its flowerless sisters.
Even borders of frostbitten
bluebirds would not stop
this inexorable March
to summer.

Recycling

My three year old draws and colors on scrap
paper clean and white, on one side only,
the other sides covered with typed words
of my unpublished novel; pages I produced
intending to market my creativity serve instead
to develop my daughter's art, her play
with space and form.
I was just admiring her day's work
when I rediscovered Chapter XXXIII, the one
where my character frets about his relative impotence
compared to his two cop brothers.
It all seemed to read pretty well,
reminding me why I thought the whole
thing might make it into a real book,
but then I could not find page 253
behind any of the drawings of faces and shapes,
the vivid greens, pinks, purples.
Maria must have torn this page apart
for some game she was playing or magic
design she made, discarding it easily,
with youth's own magic designs.

I'm glad she can't read yet,
so when more of my pages find their
way to the trash, I won't have to take
it personally: glad also her sides
of the pages have years ahead
of only applause, approval, publication
on the refrigerator, her bedroom walls,
my office, wherever, whenever
she wants.

Thirty Year Old Christmas Card from Sylvia Ramos

I was showing my four year old my baseball
cards, most dating back
to the early and mid-sixties,
some of them even worth something, in spite
of my lack of care about what mint might mean,
when we came across some oddities
in the big cardboard box: five Outer Limits cards, including
"Jelly Man Attacks" and "Clay Man's Revenge,"
a sole football card of Boston Patriot Bob Dee
I cannot recall ever owning, a bunch of get-well
cards from when I had my appendix removed, thirty
years before (several of my well-wishers now long
dead: Uncle Nick, my Godfather Sal, whose own son
Sal Jr. just died of cancer).
A few Christmas cards also remain, random
in terms of which got saved; one is from Sylvia
Ramos, says simply, "To Joe," concludes
"Love Sylvia," right maybe when she was starting
to, when I was still too shy to find a way
to cash in on that crush.
I'd live just to see her for years later,
though we never dated, though she always chose
others. I hear of her still from her brother,
my still fine friend José.
If I insisted, I could probably get back "in touch,"
receive new words sent by Sylvia, but why
so many years have passed; we've had five marriages
between us, this last one of mine took. I'll settle
instead for this relic, "Love, Sylvia," happy
my daughter is too young to wonder how those words
got mixed up with photos of once young athletes,
Clay Man's Revenge.

Expecting Songbirds

We stopped feeding the birds
because raccoons were climbing up
on the deck to feast on the spill seed,
and though the kids enjoyed seeing them
at least as much as the birds, I did not
feel safe with their teeth and claws
so close to our lives.

But my son misses his sister, off
to the grown up world of first-grade,
the baby too young to talk to him or
share his elaborate play, so we have
put the feeder up again, though
for the second day we have had no
finches, purple or gold, nor juncos
titmice, nuthatches and certainly
no cardinals nor jays bringing their color
to our weathered grey deck.

Yet my son sits, a half hour after dawn,
in the cold room next to the deck's sliding
glass door, waiting, expecting songbirds.
I tell him it might be hours, days
before they see the seed;
he is certain it will be sooner,
since he is whispering an invitation, over
and over again, a prayer of welcome.
I bring him his favorite, soft, pale blue
blanket, his lady-bug pillow,
understanding I have to comfort
such faith for as long as it takes,
for as long as it lasts.

from
My Puerto Rican Past

Learning the Dance

A child of 3, I jumped up and down
to my parents' certain approval, confident
I had the proper technique for interpreting
Danny and the Juniors' "At the Hop."
At 7 I could twist with the best
of my tolerant older brothers
and sisters; at 11 I could monkey,
frug as frenetically as any dancer
on Shin-Dig or Hullabaloo,
never suspecting the rhythm
of mortification awaiting me
a lonely year later at my best friend
José's party, when I found myself
the only one
with no spice to my salsa
no shake to my merengue,
so obviously off beat
that José's little sister Lourdes
sneered: "Damn, Joey, you can't
Latin for shit."

A first lesson in being out
of step with the rest, mis-
placed and strangely ashamed,
too many years away from hearing
Thoreau's "different drummer"
for much-needed consolation.

My Puerto Rican Past

Sylvia Ramos, Zoraida Martínez, Gloria Flores,
just mentioning your names brings me
to the brink of irredeemable loss.
Junior Normandía, Ricky Irizarry, Carlos Torres,
once my "boys," now just men who do not know
where I am, Puerto Rican-less in the small-town
middle west, far from where I knew them
in New York, farther still from my teenage
years, where a day did not pass
me without the aroma of arroz
con habichuelas, the blaring sounds of salsa,
the guttural ease of some good friend's
advice to "Cógelo suave, chico,"
the flirtation in an "Ay dios mío, Joey,"
mouthed by someone too together, really,
to need to worry about God's protection.

I speak Spanish fluently now, from years
of study; I read and write about esoteric
Argentinians like Borges and Cortázar,
so the new Puerto Rican on our Spanish
faculty is someone I could befriend,
but probably won't, knowing how impossible
it is to replace so much past.
Three times fifteen now, I cannot
recast the purity of those connections,
bring back to my life how beautiful Sylvia Ramos
looked, like love, on an endless August evening
in working-class Queens.

Luna llena

The moon was larger than any we had
ever witnessed in Queens, powerful
enough to affect more than the ocean's
tides, insistent like a prayer repeated
into effortless memory, passionate
its backdrop as I held you closer
than the space between notes of the love
song the orchestra was playing.
The full moon that night in Puerto Rico
promised us an eternity of stars,
rum and coke washed nights,
as I danced with you Sylvia, wondering
how you could not be mine,
since the very sky conspired
to convince you happiness would settle
upon us like the sea surrounds Luquillo's
white sands, if only you would say sí
to the arguments of that night's bolero.
Instead, I left without you from Fajardo,
in tired daylight, back to Long Island,
where no one really believes
how yellow, how immense, how insistent
the moonlight matters to anything
as important as what perished
that lost, lunar night: the youth
to believe your body's grace could
not lie to us, the innocence
to expect a moon that wise,
that full, could never
be wrong.

Oh, Sylvia

Puerto Rico touches you again,
its warmth graces your face,
fragrances insinuate their way
through your senses insatiate:
mangos, rain on your hair, sea wind.
Sounds revise you: far away call
of the shore birds, whistle of the coquí,
thunderclap, chords from the cuatro,
scrape of the guiro, carry you back
every bit as powerfully as the rudest
salsa orchestra. You have returned
to where you live, home, away,

remembering you were born
in a New York City hospital, grew
up in working-class Queens;
you speak English like any native
New York Puerto Rican, your child-
hood felt snow, splashed in icy
puddles, saw the snow grow grey
and die back to flowers,
roses and honeysuckle that left again.

You can return to Puerto Rico
as often as flowers fade, green
revises, coquís call; you will
never leave home you became
the moment you were born a mainland
child, grown ever more beautiful
from the grace of that embracing island
that calls you back, but can never have
you whole, away, as long as your life
continues glowing here, in mine,
fragrant, warm, alluring, sounding
through seasons: death, life,
through time.

Carlos Visits Columbus

He will be uncomfortable with all those blue eyes
one rarely sees in the South Bronx.
Fortunately, we live on South Campus,
plenty of blacks and the few Latinos
the city owns will be here to greet him.
Back home a young woman with long, black hair
and even a hint of "raza" would be enough
to set him to murmuring
or to "rapping" after beers or Sangria.
But the blonde in the string bikini
who enjoys sun daily on the apartments'
front lawn
will only unnerve him.
Both of us grateful brown skin screens embarrassment.
All those blue eyes borrow me still.

Yankees in East Texas

Beaumont smells like the pursuit of riches;
when the winds blows right
you can sense confessions of hundreds
of corporate crimes, refined not a bit
more than the petroleum we won't mind
having at the cheapest possible rates.
This constant reminder, clinging
to the not-invisible air
pollutes everyday thinking:
like the local advertisement for birth
control where the grown-up convinces
the teen not to get his girl pregnant
so he won't have a life-
time of wages garnished,
or the Chevron foreman
confessing his chagrin
over being unable to prevent
a chemical leak at the plant,
his embarrassment springing
from all the money he cost the company.

The Gulf of Mexico tries
to wash away all these sins,
pounds benedictions on the sandy shores:
alligators and lobster-like crayfish thrive
in the ditches and backwaters; fire ants
build elaborate mounds of biting
pain that dare you to step on them.
Young waitresses at local restaurants
laugh at northeastern humor and accents,
imply that New Jersey and Connecticut
crimes are just as foul, though we assure
them with our superior
smiles we at least seem
upset when refuse fouls our beaches,
colors our air, and we insist our smells
be less honest, less certainly like
the aroma of cash money down.

White Pumpkins Outside Wal-Mart

> *Or is it, that as in essence whiteness is not so much a*
> *color as the visible absence of color,*
> *and at the same time the concrete of all colors,*
> *is it for these reasons that there is such a dumb blankness,*
> *full of meaning, in a wide landscape of snows—a colorless,*
> *all-color of atheism from which we shrink?"*
> —Herman Melville, Moby Dick, Chapter XLII,
> "The Whiteness of the Whale"

They need to be orange,
everyone knows, a Fall Festival
color so many of the leaves turn to,
that final brightness before the browns
and greys of winter.

There is no innocence or purity
to a white pumpkin; it sits pale proof
of genetic engineering or something
just as sinister, since no sane person
could conceive of a white pumpkin pie.

Already we know the white of winter
snow can pretend to be a playground,
a beautiful blanket, even as it cannot keep
the secret of the earth's cold conclusions
from anyone but children.

A white pumpkin is premature
spectral cynicism, too forced
foreshadowing of what is to follow
fall: a ghost, laughing its flickering
laugh at the stomach-aches, rotting
teeth from too much
candy corn.

Woman Burning Leaves a Few Months After Her Son's Death

Killed in a car wreck
caused by his own drunken driving.
He wasn't a bad kid; he was

her only son perished half a mile from their house
in the woods, too far from the scolding
she might have given him.

The funeral finished, the relatives gone
again to their own mortalities,
she and her husband sometimes feign

a return to normalcy, a faith-based calm,
among other strategies society expects,
mostly for its own good.

And so she burns leaves left over
from autumn, from oaks who give them up
reluctantly bending to spring.

In April sunshine she stands
next to a smoldering, smoky pile
of things that once were green

to make way for the lawn,
to make way for some flowers,
to mourn her loss as common as the seasons.

Night Break

A silver white moon, wider than doubt,
stayed whole in the early light
of an all blue sky.
I could not find the yellow
of the sun, somewhere just arisen
in the east, and, as fully as I knew
it had to be the source
of how I saw that symbol of night
defiant at the edge of day,
for a moment, like leftover dreaming,
I believed it was that distant rock
shining itself into morning,
outlasting the stars,
dawning past the limits
of darkness.

The Banker Does Not Smile On His Way to Work

On my separate way to a job I enjoy,
I see him, cold in his three piece suit
without overcoat for the brief walk
from his silver Mercedes.
In that short space I catch him
scowling at the bits of slush
on Italian shoes, in anticipation
of the many moribund mortgages,
IRAs without revolt, music-less CDs,
other unqualified applications of his
banker's hours day.
His eyes, when he thinks no one watches,
are not the farmer's friend, could not
value less my patronage, nor can they
reflect a sense of any worthy work
to be done in that stone building,
where the old Savings & Loan finally limped
into the conglomerate arms
of the teal-logoed Bank Midwest.

I do not care to sit in judgment,
I do not search for a stone to cast,
I wish instead the banker had a happy
or at least ironic look, instead
of the self-contempt he seems to send out
with the steam from his perhaps flu-bound
cough, from which he knows too well
no overcoat nor careful galoshes
could have saved him.

New Neighbors

"but thou shall love thy neighbor as thyself. I am the Lord."
—Leviticus, 19:18

The mother, aggressively blue-eyed, loquacious and proud
of it, brags how she sometimes is hard
to take.

She, her Japanese husband, five nice-looking kids
and an off-white cockatiel have come to Kirksville
for a local church where they promise she will be
"celebrated, not just tolerated."

About every fifth sentence
she mentions the Lord.
He talks to her all the time,
told her it was His will for her
to take this up-scale house
in our middle-class neighborhood
in the woods, when she had worried
He'd want them to bring joy to some shack.

I wonder why He didn't warn her about me,
not the Lord-on-my-speed-dial type,
not one to celebrate someone wanting
to pawn off her worldly wants
as God's will.

I guess one of us just isn't praying
hard enough.

Dulcinea at Pancake City

"I have dreamed thee too long,
never seen thee nor touched thee, but loved
thee with all of my heart."
—*"Dulcinea," Man of La Mancha, Leigh and Darien*

The musical they made of Cervantes' Don Quixote
has Dulcinea certain, as female lead.
Crazy Don's pure belief in her goodness,
in spite of her strumpety past
transforms her, eventually, even taking her voice
from husky whore's to sweet-toned soprano
by the show's finale.

But in Cervantes' Don Quixote
Dulcinea never shows.
Sure, Don imagines some kitchen wench
named Aldonza for his dream woman, but he never
says an actual word to either one of them
for the whole one thousand and fifty page opus,
never gives the actual woman a chance
to agree to the name change.

What this must mean to us here, now, in 2004,
thousands of miles and lives away
from 16th century Spain, is that almost anyone
might be Dulcinea. Say, for example,
this sad-grey-eyed waitress at the twenty-four hour
diner, who was young once, maybe, who so clearly
is not enjoying her job, yet still finds
her path pointing towards politeness,
even as she appreciates your own efforts
at chivalry.

Yes, she just might find a way to be transfigured,
to stop being just Jolene,
if only you could be insane enough
to ride with her towards a moment of belief,
she crazy enough to sing you
back her song.

Better Off

I hear you made your newly-wed slaughter pigs
just to start to pay off the many thousands
you owe on your too many credit cards,
but later sent him packed
back to his Momma in La Plata
so you could flirt more effectually
with your graduate advisor,
who you almost made, until
your sexy sister, barely
eighteen, who had moved to Ohio
just to be near you, took your place
as his mistress, the plane ticket
to Portugal, for a year's ride
on his Fullbright.
Our mutual friends who relay your
latest misadventures smile over
the phone, smugly certain how lucky
I must feel you escaped me, what a favor
you did turning down my offer to gather
all your problems on my silly shoulders,
one easy payment you would be sure
always to make on time.
I know they are right
to applaud you as past
tense in my life,
every bit as fully as I understand
you could have given me nothing
more than the misery your light
brown eyes promised,
but through all these intervening
years, I've never stopped wondering
what I might have been willing
to slaughter for the chance
to keep you here.

Reunion Cathedral Prep

High school for "priest faggots,"
young "Poindexters" who prefer virgin
Mary to some maybe-willing Margaret, inept
athletes, their rosaries no protection
against the pummeling they took on ball
fields against Christ the King,
Holy Cross, Archbishop Molloy.

These impressions of our peers
we lived with uncomfortably
for four years of inordinate drinking,
cursing, female chasing to disprove
the stereotype we also feared.

Now that most of us are married,
have children, we no longer
apologize for that place
we spent the brunt of our teenage years.
Lawyers, doctors, cops, contractors,
our success leaves unquestioned
why we placed ourselves where priests
are first manufactured. We got out
before it was too late to prove
we were men, once crazy
enough to believe
in the Messianic, fully normal enough
now to wonder how we ever
preferred a Blessed
mother to even the most ordinary
Margaret.

The Bachelorette

My wife waits all week for the show, so
I will watch too, with the remote ready
to check the Knicks' game during ads,
giving me full license to ridicule

the fifteen guys left,
all of them primping for Meredith,
the Portland model and make-up artist,
who, "earlier on 'The Bachelor,'"

chose to skip her grandmother's
funeral not to miss her chance
with bachelor Bob, who dumped her
mostly because all the talk

about corpse grandma was a downer.
But now it's Meredith's turn
to choose from lawyers, business
owners and no fewer than three

pushy fellows in pharmaceutical sales.
There' s something so sick about TV
offering us reality: what could be more
phony than all these pretenders

thinking they might marry Meredith,
except maybe the one who actually will,
except Meredith's own motivations,
except me pretending I don't want to watch.

Villanelle
(Inspired by a "double Villanelle" performed by a prominent poet)

Hitler was a bad man.
He murdered gypsies, Slavs and Jews
"Hitler was a very bad man,"

the poet declared, as if it were news
we hadn't heard or wouldn't understand
Hitler was a bad man.

The poet declaimed fearlessly as if he had nothing to lose,
like only a black-vested, purple-silk shirted seer can:
"Hitler was a very bad man."

And why not, this poet had paid his dues,
had every right to judge, take this noble stand—
Hitler was a bad man.

His audience enthralled, not one inclined to snooze,
his insight into evil as natural as his tan,
"Hitler was a very bad man."

Afterwards, amidst the French cheese and the booze,
subject and poet blurred together for one fan:
Hitler was a bad man?
"Hitler was a very bad man"?

May 31, 1989

"Maybe it is you yourself now really ushering me to the true songs."
—Walt Whitman, "Goodbye My Fancy"

It's Walt Whitman's birthday
so I should write a poem.

He'd be 170, maybe is
somewhere, better
greyer than ever.
I like to think whenever I sense
lilacs, he senses them too,
when I view the moon hanging
half-an-hour high we both relive
the sweet hell within, children
again, once more.
I like to believe
I cannot sing a song myself
without him hearing it,
cannot cross into Brooklyn
or remember Rockaway Beach
is part of Paumanok, that fish-
shaped Long Island without
conjuring him up as real as
any phantom on these
crowded streets, still,
sandy beaches.
I remember he asked me,
"Who knows but I am enjoying this?
who knows, for all the distance, but I am as good as
looking at you now, for all you cannot see me?"
What a comfort, to believe eternity
need not dismantle death to maintain
its own integrity, what a comfort
to enjoy birthdays so many years
after we have said Good-
bye to our fancy.

My Wife Laughs In Her Sleep

Sometimes a girlish giggle,
more often a longer, lilting laugh.
Not the kind a good joke generates,
more a vote of self-confidence,
liquid notes to anyone listening:
I am very happy to be who I am.

My wife sleeps soundly, snores
moments after her head hugs
the pillow, never returning
to the real world until sunlight.
It's as if she can't wait
to get to those dreams
where she is so full
of her control.

Hardly a coincidence, the dreams I've had
of her betrayals, and the casual way
she miniskirts blame,
remorseless as a leopard.

It doesn't help to awake
from such dreams to the sound
of her laughter ringing
its warning in the unbroken darkness:
how I had better be aware
of her every waking moment.

That Day They Mugged My Mother

...was a blue-sky spring day of flowers'
fragrances undone by the smell
of becoming-ghetto garbage and sweaty
fear from all the possible victims of violence.

She was on the last leg of the five block
gauntlet from the Q41 bus to our modest home,
when two teens attacked, though only one
grabbed for her purse,

the other stood back, new to stealing
or appalled by his partner's easy transition
from schoolyard to crime scene, plus
my mother hit back, screamed with the righteousness

of the wronged, got the better
of her assailant, was giving her
the purse in a way that teen never
intended, hitting her so hard

the witness mugger pleaded, "Stop, please,
leave her alone!" but my mother kept
swinging, tried to hold that young
woman for the police to counsel,

but Angelo the ice cream man could not
get his tired white truck to fly fast enough
to aid my mother, so the couple got
away, though, certainly, they

were too ashamed to try our part
of the neighborhood again, if not
fully cured from a life of crime
by the hammering their sense of the world took

that day they mugged my mother,
a day she claimed back the simplicity
of apple blossoms, the fragrance of lilacs,
other trees and bushes mistaken

for co-conspirators, cover for criminals,
when, really, they were always innocent, natural
as my mother's refusal to cower, while her right hand
owned the force of a very heavy purse.

Driving to a Poetry Reading in My Father-in-Law's Pick-Up Truck

The tire was flat, nothing could be done
on Sunday morning in Palmyra, MO,
except accept the offer of a truck.
Although at first I couldn't make it run,
some more foot on the gas got me to go
towards St. Louis, cursing my stupid luck.
Never before had I been so above
most other drivers on the open road,
never before the kinds of peer-like looks
from truck guys with no clue I write of love
and loss in poems, since this thing I drove
was more persona than you'll find in books.
And so my reading had more force by far,
than any I had gotten to by car.

Claire Calling Me

I pick up the phone at work
expecting some excuse from a late-paper
student, a reminder about a meeting.
Instead I get, "Hi, Daddy," from
the three year old voice of my daughter,
"I found my green watering can,"
the one we couldn't locate anywhere
last afternoon when we wanted to water
the seeds we'd placed the first
really warm day of spring.

We only talked a half minute more,
but the rest of my Monday
resounded Claire's little voice
anxious to share the blessing
of her day, which she did,
every minute of the rest of mine.

The Light in the Kitchen

In my parents' kitchen,
in the house they have inhabited
for fifty years, where my mother
has prepared at least fifteen thousand suppers,
the light has always come from well above,
through two long, fluorescent bulbs activated
by a hard pull on a dangling string.

For fifty years my father, eighty-four this April,
has handled all maintenance of that essential light,
from changing the tricky bulbs to redoing undone wiring.
Yet its latest outage, during our Christmas visit,
my father could not fix.

At the top of a stepladder,
both of them unsteady with age,
my father tries again and again
to get the bulbs back to glowing,
but the switch just makes the bulbs flicker,
no matter how much he adjusts, tightens,
no matter how hard or often he tugs
on the strings.
Even the bulbs rebel; half a dozen times
one or the other slips out
and my father or I (once more his inept assistant
after so many years absent from the role) have to catch
the rods before they can find the floor and shatter.

My father's breath becomes labored,
his frustration uttered in Italian curses,
his embarrassment more muted, though plain
to me, even while his wife of almost sixty years
more vocally frets from fear in front of her
puzzled grandchildren, far too young
to credit her panic attacking over
those long familiar cylinders refusing
to work for my father, me
standing below trying to catch, hold,
send back
the kitchen's light.

Buying Seeds

We've got four pathetic azalea bushes
in a sad sort of circle in the center
of our yard. Despite years of neglect,
they are merely moribund, not deceased;
last time I looked, each of them still held
some green leaves, were stubborning their way
into another spring.

Though I hate our too large lawn,
have long since resigned it to the moles,
I never have turned completely away
from flowering. Our forsythias and redbuds,
also unkillable, are now full
of yellow and purple fire. They prod
me to put Miracle Grow on the too long
Wal-Mart list.

I find some specifically for azaleas,
other "acid-loving" plants:
medium blue crystals to mix with water.
Once I'm in the neighborhood,
I find myself drawn to all
the seeds on sale.
We've never had much luck
with those packets, either, but the kids
don't seem to mind. Every spring they want
to help sow some; every summer are delighted
with whatever is willing to appear.

So I get columbine, aster, foxglove
and a big canister of wildflower mix.
Later, when I go to give the azaleas
their drink of sky, I find,
not quite obscured by the oak leaf litter,
one plant already with two bright buds,
against all kinds of odds, sense,
as if anticipating, collaborating
my still good intentions.

from
Tough Guys Don't Write

Like In a Western...

vultures, riding low and black
against a sapphire sky
seem to be following me
as I attempt to walk off
my latest arrhythmia.

I live in the woods:
they've probably just spotted
some sick possum or road-killed
raccoon, plus I'm usually back in sinus
rhythm minutes after one of these walks.

Still, in what western did the guy
on his way through the desert
not think he'd be just fine too?
All I need now is the cattle skull
to predict how this picture will end.

Tough Guys Don't Write

Posers from Hemingway to Junot,
from Bukowski to Eminem have never fooled
folks with any sense, anyone who's ever
really met an actual bad ass.

The real deal hardly ever reflects
and never in tranquility,
doesn't take the time to find words
to express what he always finds expressible
with a fist or a blade or a gun.

I'm not saying a writer can't be mean
and almost anyone can abuse drugs
or sometimes win a fight,
but there's a reason writers
want you to know they once
worked construction, survived
the 'hood, didn't dodge
a purple heart;

there's a reason really tough
women and men can always pull
the writer from a line-up
of purported thugs,
scars or sneers notwithstanding.

As soon as you're ready
to write a novel,
rap yourself into a sonnet,
stage your life for all the world,
you forever after can only
posture not to care
what others might think
or feel.

Joseph Sr.

This photo of my father, behind me
as I write, reminds me of where I came
from: Italian, working class. Dad's dark eyes
hawk's nose, neat grey mustache, tough-guy-non-smile
confess to all the books my students see—
Leaves of Grass, Ficciones, The Name
of the Rose at least a little belied—
a janitor's son, no matter the miles,
the money, the time. But the bright ones may
suspect, I'm far from worried when they sight
the resemblance. Only my own design
placed the picture there, where, everyday
my father looks over whatever I write,
while my view holds books, unless I look behind.

Frankie

My brother Frank, nine years older,
had to do the things with me
my dad was too tired for—like my first
movie, "The Guns of Navarone"—war
at the Lefferts Theater on Liberty—nine
long blocks in a bad neighborhood—Frankie, in his black
leather jacket, whose pockets I knew hid both brass knuckles
and a switch blade: I could try to stay in step anywhere
with him.

My first time fishing, off the bridge at Broad Channel,
I almost caught the day's biggest flounder, till it
escaped my hook three quarters of the way up and out
of Jamaica Bay, splashing me down to defeat. Frank gave me
a rare smile of commiseration, kept emphasizing the size
over the loss.

A few years earlier he'd taken me for my first real haircut,
at Bruno's barbershop, with its glass bottles of brightly colored
hair tonics, Bruno, with his Italian accent intact
after fifty years absence from Palermo.
Frank had promised me I could get a "flat-top," like him,
but when I proudly told Bruno, he eyed Frank
for confirmation, and my older brother said, "Sorry, kid,
Ma don't want you looking like that." I had to settle
for the conventional, "wish I had a watermelon" crew.
I wanted to cry, but inside I knew she was right:
I wasn't ever going to be anything
like Frankie.

Mushrooms

I

She has never liked the texture, my wife,
the rubbery feel on the tongue.
It isn't the way they taste,
but how.

I argue some cheap ones in a Wal-
Mart can can't compare to close-
to-magical morels, buttery portabellos,
but my wife wants nothing to do
with edible fungus, figures
they're all too close to disease,
is not a bit surprised most of their cousins
are poisonous, nor that the atomic bomb
plumes a massive cloud, mushroom shaped
and fatal.

II

There are places with miles of mushrooms
growing underground, mushrooms sporing
on trees, mushrooms pink as puberty,
yellow as gold.
There are grey, brown and black ones,
mushrooms that stink worse than lies.
We had this one network of torpedo shaped
toadstools, with an aggressive odor
like someone else's sex
multiply on our mulch pile. I tried
to pull them up by their stalks, but
they returned. I had to get under
the mulch where there were purple veins,
fatty, squishy bulbs. I thought I was done
with them twice, but the grey-white phallic-
faced reminders of my own mortality would rise
again, making me suddenly more certain than
my wife, even, of the evil texture
of their intent.

Fishing With Fernando

We took the Q21 to Broad Channel,
got off at the first bridge, bought
sand worms, had our hopes far flung
to the water below, where flounder, eel, maybe
other ocean answers awaited us.

Fernando was trying to decide
whether to head for Fajardo,
to try to convince his one-time
fiancée Sylvia not to forget
their future just because
the Ramos clan had abandoned
Queens the summer before.

I had lost that same Sylvia
to Fernando a few summers earlier,
never fully forgotten the fantasy
where she would come to her senses
and see me as meant for far more
than friendship.

And yet, as he and I interrupted
our conversation with the occasional fish,
as we saw afternoon slip reliably towards evening,
as we scoured the bridge for a few extra worms
left by people with more decided lives,
admired the sun setting the horizon
to more colors than we ever saw normal
twilights in our sea-less neighborhood,

I found myself convinced Fernando
deserved his chance, wished much more
for him than the joys we two
could scare up together:
some smelly fish, cardboard boxes
gritty, one last lonely
worm among them,
on the darkening bridge.

My Parents' Backyard

"The place is a total wreck. The weeds are so high you can't see the few flowers that are left—it's like a freakin' jungle. The garage is cavin' in, the sidewalk's crumblin', and the neighbors have a bunch a their crap in our yard because the fence has caved in. It's gotta be the worst yard in Queens."
—from a phone conversation with my sister, Annmarie

The German lady used to give us peaches
from her tree that leaned almost into our property
over the pretty picket fence. Flowers for three seasons
surrounded the sidewalks Dad himself had poured.
Red roses climbed the walls of the light green garage,
their yellow, orange, pink cousins looking up
at them from every direction.
In the very back our apple tree, beside the fig bush
and slender pear, whose hard fruit flavored us
right off the tree.
Somehow there was room for a see-
saw, slide, swing-set, and, just behind the garage,
a vegetable plot serving tomatoes, lettuce, cucumbers,
squash throughout the later summer.
I remember soaring
on the yellow swing, surrounded
by produce, flowers, fruit,
knowing nothing
of death, decay,
as my feet seemed bathed in blue
sky, cottony white clouds.

Who Names Their Kid Brandi?

The Sherwoods did, having to know
a name like that made their daughter
far more likely a future Miss Idaho
than philosophy Professor or M.D.

Of course, as one of "Barker's Beauties"
she hasn't needed much Kierkegaard
or organic chemistry, and now Drew Carey
gives her a little more air time, even.

Plus, there was the made-for-TV movie
with the sharks, and Brandi's body, so meant
for a swimsuit, those large, light eyes
so clearly for cameras.

Ph.D. me, I confess, when my wife's out
there's almost no one with whom
I'd rather waste my life
on summer reruns.

I wonder if she has a web
site. I wonder if she'd
appreciate
a poem.

Watching Dracula With My Daughter

The Lugosi one, from the early '30's:
hardly any blood, Renfield's eyes
crazier than the idea of a living dead,
Mina not any more grateful to be rescued
from the Count than she should be.

I send my younger two off to play,
mostly so my wife won't blame me
for five year old Claire's nightmares,
but Maria, twelve, stays with me to watch
the horror unfold.

All the darkness, the black and white
castles, crypts, bats we watch together,
laughing at what is supposed to be frightening,
since that is what we always do
best together.

I thought I wanted Maria to watch with me
because we love the classics I watched
with my sisters when I was her age,
but this is not the Marx Brothers
or some old, romantic comedy.

At its core, this version of the vampire
shows a father worried about his daughter's
well-being but unaware until almost too late
of the imminence of her peril. Not even
the bite marks on her neck are enough to alert him,

not even Mina's best friend's demise
with its post-mortem menacing of little children
in the park at dusk. And about as late I recognize
how perverse it will seem to my spouse,
off to her women's meeting

that Maria and I should be viewing
the work of Dracula together,
to observe how close he comes to stealing
the life of someone's young daughter,
straight through to the end, when

the stake is being driven through
the Count's cold heart,
even though the old films never keep
on screen those awful things we know
are necessary, finally, to a drama's resolution.

Watching West Side Story With Maria

My daughter, age twelve, who used to "sing" along
to my singing of her song when she was still a baby.

I had to remind her there were sad parts,
just like Romeo and Juliet is beautiful but sad.

She loved "Officer Krupke" and other bits of comedy,
adored the dancing, harmony, her father's New York streets.

But Maria wasn't ready for Chino shooting Tony down
into Maria's arms; she seemed shocked by the loss.

In spite of my warnings, Maria seemed to be wondering
why her Dad would have wanted her to see this,

seemed uncertain how she could continue to be
the same girl she was before the movie;

all my words about the positive message,
the ultimate triumph of love over hate

falling on still stunned ears,
eyes close to tears.

How could a musical be so sad?
How could the good guy end up dead on the dirty street,

after all that pretty music, lovely, loving
lonely Marias in the world?

Little Girls In Their Easter Dresses Sitting Atop A Cannon

"Where have all the flowers gone, long time passing?"
—Pete Seeger

They are posing for a picture,
two sisters, maybe five and three,
floral prints, long, light-brown hair,
certain smiles.

It is Easter Sunday morning, after church
and before the holiday ham with their grandparents.
Their mother, back for a small town visit, thinks
it is precious to prop her daughters on the Civil War

cannon, landmark greeting,
in front of Rotary Park, commemorating
the skirmish enough death dignified to call
the Battle of Kirksville.

They smile the smile of little children welcoming
warm April sunshine, buoyed by the magical
appearance of chocolate bunnies, marshmallow
chicks in pastel baskets. Innocents who have yet to learn

someone is always dying for our sins.

Mango Memory

My first time on an airplane
I flew all the way to San Juan,
where José, Sylvia, Fernando were
waiting to take me back with them
to Fajardo, where Fernando would finish
off my fantasy by marrying José's sister, Sylvia.

We'd all grown up together in Queens,
until the Ramos family headed back
to their homeland after José finished
high school, and soon after Fernando
fled his Sylvia-less life to join them.

Two days before the wedding, we went
to pick mangoes and avocados on Monte Brisas,
at an orchard managed by a family friend.
Fernando, always braver than I,
climbed high upon a mango tree and shook
big branches for the best fruit. Several of us
below harvested what was falling.

Sylvia saw one missile aiming for my head,
pushed me aside to take it full
on her shoulder. It raised a bruise we worried
would show through her white wedding gown.
It wasn't two years later she left Fernando
for another man. She's now, José tells me,
with husband number four.

My children like mangoes a lot,
so I bring them home, even though
these Wal-Mart impostors can't compare
to the sun-warmed freshness of one
from a Puerto Rican tree, even though
I can never cut into their pulpy
yellow-orange flesh, sense their tropic
perfume without thinking of Sylvia Ramos,
so many mangoes later, still pushing me
away for my own good.

Mango Street Rules

Most of my students reading Cisneros' classic
will marvel at how an author
from so much poverty and prejudice
could travel to such success, via her work
we read from junior high through college.

I see some of that too, plus I admire
the actual writing, though the part where Esperanza
spends five bucks just to have her fortune told
only makes me laugh, since, at that age (and I'm
almost exactly Cisneros' age)

I never had five dollars of my own to waste
where I grew up, South Jamaica, Queens, a neighborhood
more dangerous than Sandra's mythical Mango,
especially for me, the last white boy left, praying
for amigos on streets owned by Dominicans and Puerto Ricans.

Even worse, now, as a grown up blanco,
I can't get any acclaim for the success I had in making
it out of the barrio. I'm not even allowed to call it a barrio;
I'm not even allowed to compare my lot to sister Cisneros;
I'm not even allowed to write this poem.

Hallene's Christmas Call

My wife answered the phone,
so the surprise of your voice
in my December was disallowed.
And talking to you in a living
room crowded with opened presents,
the noise of four children navigating them,
left little room for anything but small
talk. What big thing could we say
now decades since I whiffed on the chance
to put up a tree, rainbowed with lights,
annual ornaments, silvered with tinsel,
and you beside me every early winter.

The more you refuse to neglect me,
like you sometimes did, in the fullness
of your dark-flowered beauty,
the more I'm held to my desire
for the kind of longing a long-settled
sort can hardly even admit to missing.
And I do miss you, Hallene,
without remedy, since even if calls were
more frequent or we really did get together
with our respective families in tow
this summer, there is no way to ornament
loss that can make what might have been
ever be, in the winter of this again
that never was.

Summer Night Sky with Margaret

She's not even two, so no sense
sending her eyes up to search for the Summer
Triangle: "Look at all those stars," is invitation enough.
These balmy nights, Margaret in my arms,
while one hand tries to hold on to the dog's leash,
I have to negotiate the darkness carefully,
never knowing when our schnauzer might pull
after some white tailed deer or red fox she's sent scurrying
into the woods. It's worth the awkward walking to witness
Margaret listening for a barred owl's call,
looking to see what size the moon has decided to be,
if it isn't playing hide and seek too well behind the clouds.
On the way back in, we always check on our shadows
as they darkly play with our sizes, shapes against the little shed.
Back inside, Margaret's ready to report
to her mother and siblings all of what she saw and heard:
the yellow half-moon, her favorite blue stars,
the songs of crickets, frogs, the crazy croaking I told her
was a coon. Her teenage brother asks if she saw any coyotes,
and she laughs, though we've heard their howls before,
because it's funny to Margaret, the idea of having to worry
out there, with the early August moon and stars,
high up in her father's arms.

from
Ode To Pears
(Uncollected Published Poems)

Ode To Pears

"Siempre
eres nueva como nada
o nadie,
siempre
recién caída
del Paraíso.
—Pablo Neruda, "Oda a la manzana"

Because you only rarely grace
a pie or cake or juice container,
or lend your gold-green flavor
to a gum-drop or jar of jam,
you find no place at the core
of most people's consciousness, crowded
with apples, oranges and grapes.

But whether hard but penetrable,
as life is, green Bartlett,
(enrobed sometimes in red)
or the soft surrender
of your ripeness poached in Port
(or better still to let your yellowed lusciousness
pour out by itself, like wine)
who cannot sniff out God in your aroma?
Who deny the miracle of the cross

fertilization of what your so dark brown seeds
bare to the earth, that story of eventual fruition,
the glory of the orchard or modest backyard
blessed with pear-shaped promise,
with the very intoxication of hunger
into love. Let the devil keep privileging his apple;
only a demon doesn't desire
the knowledge of a pear.

After Realizing My Mother Had Been Cursing All Along In Italian

She was always such a saint
lover: Anthony would find her lost
keys; Cosmos and Damian take turns
quelling any fever one of her seven children carried;
Lucy easing her eye strain long hours she labored.

Sure, she'd lose her temper, yell at us a lot,
even an occasional hand slap, but I'd never hear
her curse. Dad wasn't bad that way himself,
left the F-bombs at the construction sites
(once, age sixteen, I felt a coming-of-age

when he let loose a "Cocksucker!" the time
just the two of us kept trying to get my absent brother-
in-law's car alarm to shut up), but from my mother
not even the "Bullshit!" or "God damn it!" Dad
and the other parents let loose without even a first

thought. I emulated my mother, stood out
from my friends for refusing to tie my manhood
to how many filthy words I could fling back at them
(though I did still manage once to send Ricky Irizarry
home crying without laying either a hand or so

much as a single "Shithead!" on him.) So, imagine
my chagrin when I finally found out what "Cazzo!"
or "Vaffancul'!" meant, words my mother rolled out
more often than her rosary beads, violent
benedictions making her human after all,

though too late to do me any good.

Mr. Normandía

played stickball with the teens at P.S. 121,
fastballing so hard we'd see the old chalk
puff, a baby-blue ghost off the brick
strike zone and onto the Pensy Pinkie.

His aqua eyes as devil's bright
as his son Junior's, making us think
our fathers must only be old
by choice.

Forty years later he sits at his front porch
as I walk my wife and four children
past his house a Sunday
towards St. Teresa's.

I thought my parents the only old
timers on the block still unwilling
to bow to The Grim Reaper, or
his look-alike cousin, The Nursing Home,

but after Mass in the same church
where I weekly altar-boyed, before
graduating to getting back just
once a year,

he's still there, so I say, "Mr. Normandía,
it's me, Joey, Junior's friend,"
and it takes him a moment but then
the blue lights are back on

and he can't get over how much my kids
look like me. I can't believe Junior's dead
eight years and my having conjured our days together
for all that time with the double spectres of death and memory.

I hate to return my dead friend's father
so soon to his present Sunday
paper, am surprised a week later to hear my
four year old saying to herself, "Mr. Normandía,

Mr. Normandía," a chant that is part of some
elaborate game she's invented from her NY trip,
something she plays by herself, in so far as any child
can be alone with her father's phantoms.

After Jumper Died

and he was already in fairly full rigor
before we found him, lying stiff in the dank basement
where he slept his final sleep,
I helped my father carry him out
to the trunk of our light green Dodge Dart,

so Dad could drive our dead dog to the ASPCA
office and dispose of Jumper's seven plus years
as our fairly faithful collie, before disposing
of me at high school baseball practice on a Saturday
morning of a cold March in Queens.

I got dropped off a little sooner than necessary
so was already dressed for practice and sitting morose
in front of my locker, saddened to lose one of my few
steady friends. When my teammates drifted in,
seeing how overcome I seemed and wondering, "What's

the matter, Benny?" I simply sighed, "My dog died."
They started laughing, uproariously, about uncontrollably,
and I looked in shock and close to shouted, "No, he really died,"
and they roared all the more, certain it was just another
of my gags, and the best one in some time.

It took tears, almost, to convince them Jumper
really was a corpse, and then they offered
as sincere condolences as teens are capable
of for their 1st baseman's deceased dog and I decided,
from that almost-spring morning forward, I'd better

not make a joke out of just about everything anymore.

After I Couldn't Grind With Sylvia Ramos

in Kerry Cannon's basement, his cut-up-glow-paper walls
surrounding us with so many smug stars
and planets, while the Friends of Distinction slow-sung
"Going in Circles" to emphasize the irony: I a freshman
at Cathedral Prep in a dark room recognizing

no priesthood beyond what I might
sanctify by pressing Sylvia's present
willingness tight through me, hoping to claim
her beauty my birthright, while all my important peers
stood evaluating, envious, even those

similarly enclosed in the desperation
of their own accountings, since Sylvia
was the finest flower in our particular
mud puddle, yet somehow favored me,
one of the least of our brethren.

So who could be surprised when I fanned
the at-bat, turned the required movements
of almost indifferent lust into a tepid,
troubled waltz, as I tried stepping out
of the neighborhood, the world, with my high-

blown regard for my dance partner
intact. Instead we held close only my certain shame,
Sylvia forbidden to me forever after
my clumsy cancelling of any chance
I might have clutched even to pretend

I could ever be hard enough for this grind.

Birthday Drum

On the way to the secluded hole on the Chariton
we see three vultures, black and red on
an abandoned barn, try not to believe
in bad omens.

This spot we now approach a friend recommended,
the same one who took us night catfishing
with an almost guarantee of lunkers,
ending with our usual, habitual disappointments.

The descent to the river is steep.
We navigate brambles and poison ivy, as
we stumble down. There is even garbage
to get through, further to test our time.

Once we have worms in the water
we are alone with our wishes,
my older daughter Maria and I hoping fervently for Joey,
our fishing fanatic on his eleventh birthday.

He catches a channel as tiny as a minnow,
but his smile has no irony;
he has never caught a catfish before,
declares the trip already a success.

Five minutes later he is not smiling,
but pulling steady, reeling slowly,
against something that almost negates his effort,
pulls against him big.

I'm far off down the shore,
but walk quickly towards him and his sister
nervous to give myself over once more
to a childlike pattern of hope.

And when the fish gets close enough
to see, we realize it's a drum,
which means it might as well be a mermaid,
the way its promise takes hold.

We have no net, but I am
ready to walk in the water, certain
today should be finally the one we got;
our bucket just nabs the fish on my second try.

A nine pound drum, silvery,
with a humped back, for the three
of us to admire, release,
believe for my beaming son's birthday,

for the rest of our lives.

After Finding Out I Looked Just Like a Disney Villain

to my son's friend Mason,
who needed to write an essay on something
from his childhood most frightening,
which was me, with my "long, thin face"
like Snow White's stepmother or Scar,

my large, piercing, dark eyes, the black
and white beard, deep voice and "that thick
New York accent," as out of place here
as poor little Mason might have been, nightmarishly
lost on the mean streets of Queens, where I once lurked.

How am I supposed to show
my frightening face any more in this small
town, wondering which present tykes
and toddlers I'm terrifying, which easy laugh
might be mistaken for a diabolical guffaw?

How can I venture to the playground,
the pre-school, Wal-Mart, even, with my pretty
little princess Margaret, knowing the other children
are thanking their fairy godmothers
not to have been cursed with such a sire?

My four children know better; seventeen year old
Joey laughed long over what Mason confessed.
Still, maybe I should just stay inside,
in what will have to pass for a castle,
so I can hoard my true, inner beauty only for them,

like some dragon guarded treasure.

After Discovering I Was the Only One in My Neighborhood Not To Own a Chainsaw

Not a tornado, the thunderstorm
had sustained 70 mph winds, so lots
of old oaks broke big branches
all over our woodsy subdivision.
Hackberry Trail was blocked

for half a day, the power stayed away
for two. All over the dangerous whir of chain saws,
some even manned by women, attacking,
managing the hard wood into future fires.
Me, I had to hire

the guy who usually mows our lawn
to bring his sons and saws
to get the branches, some big as small trees,
off our circle drive and our sidewalk
leading inside.

My wife deciding she'd like
to keep the few biggest logs
safely placed to the side
for our kids to climb on, the men
drag them with their pickup and a chain

making ugly ruts through the still wet yard,
lasting evidence of how I stood at the window
watching while all my neighbors were outside,
ready, toothed tools in hand
to clear a path

towards my chronic incompetence.

Now Vanishing

The water of La Plata lake is so clear
this morning, the big bass who goes for
my golden spoon I view like a photo
from Field & Stream.
Some things are best left unseen;
I botch setting the hook,
feel the fish's disappearance
through my limp line.

I say to my fishing fanatic
fifteen year old, as we drive
back home, someday we'll
look back on all these leisurely
times and wonder where
they went. He nods, he knows,
but that truth can't touch him yet
like it does me.

His older sister is looking at colleges,
may move out of state soon.
Once she goes we'll never have
the six of us together as a full time
family again, no matter how many Christmas
times they manage to make it back from some
place more compelling than Kirksville.

I see this too, like an image
in the digital camera
I still somehow have yet
to get a feel for, a photo
I will lose forever,
like the big fish who flees, vanished
ghost who never may offer
a second opportunity.

After All

I find myself mouthing the same
words over and over, the song of my regret
in the middle of my mistrusting thankfulness
for all the calamity I have
so very far been spared.

For I have made a pact with a God
I do not love enough not to believe in:
if I continue in the far right lane
of loss, getting there slowly
and without surprise,

I will almost gratefully accept
all my defining failures: mediocre
levels of achievement, recognition, income;
the inability to love any woman
wholly and well; the middle-class hypocrisy

of my level of compassion for the poor;
the languishing of my days professing to know
more than my many students would ever guess
I don't, in this tired, small town, so far
from the broken promise of my past, and I will long

to believe my children
will figure me out sufficiently to make
fewer of these mistakes which are not
inevitable, while still maintaining sympathy
enough to keep loving at least

some silver haired vestige of my golden intent.

A Writer's Bio

Joe Benevento received a B.A. degree from NYU in English and Spanish (magna cum laude, Phi Beta Kappa), an M.A. in English from Ohio State and a Ph.D. in English from Michigan State. Benevento is Professor of English at Truman State U, where he teaches creative writing, American literature and Mystery. He is the longtime, co-editor of the Green Hills Literary Lantern.

Benevento's poems, stories, essays and reviews have appeared in about 300 places, including: Poets & Writers, The Chattahoochee Review, Pearl, Wisconsin Review, Inkwell, South Dakota Review, RE: Arts & Letter and Bilingual Review. His work has three times been nominated for Pushcart Prizes. In 1991 he was featured in a special issue of The MacGuffin, "New Decade, New Writers."

Benevento's books include three novels, two full length poetry volumes, two poetry chapbooks, and a book of short stories. They are, *Holding On*, Warthog Press, 1996; *Willing To Believe*, Timberline Press, 2003; *The Odd Squad*, Behler Publications, 2005 (a finalist for the 2006 John Gardner Fiction Book Award); *My Puerto Rican Past*, Ginninderra Press, 2006; "Tough Guys Don't Write," Finishing Line Press, 2011; *The Monsignor's Wife*, Moonshine Cove Press, 2013; and *Saving St. Teresa*, Black Opal Books, 2015.

Acknowledgments

This volume of poetry is made up primarily of selections from my four previously published volumes and chapbooks, though the final ten poems are from published poems which have not previously been collected.

Holding On, Warthog Press, West Orange, New Jersey, 1996, 78 pages

Willing To Believe, Timberline Press, Fulton, Missouri, 2003, 37 pages

My Puerto Rican Past, Ginninderra Press, Charnwood, Australia, 2006, 73 pages

Tough Guys Don't Write, Finishing Line Press, Georgetown, Kentucky, 2011, 29 pages

"Ode to Pears," *Sleet, Inkwell*
"After Realizing My Mother Had Been Cursing All Along in Italian," *I-70 Review*
"Mr. Normandía," *Concho River Review*
"After Jumper Died," *Rockhurst Review*
"After I Couldn't Grind With Sylvia Ramos," *The Potomac*
"After Finding Out I Looked Just Like a Disney Villain," *2 River View*
"After Discovering I Was the Only One in My Neighborhood Not to Own a Chainsaw," *Naugatuck River Review*
"Now Vanishing," *Bluestem*
"After All," *The Mochila Review*

CPSIA information can be obtained at www.ICGtesting.com
Printed in the USA
BVOW05s1932210815

414025BV00001B/19/P